Plants

Kate Walker

Marshall Cavendish
Benchmark
New York

Other Marshall Cavendish Offices: Marshall Cavendish International (Asia) Private Limited, 1 New Industrial Road, Singapore 536196 • Marshall Cavendish International (Thailand) Co Ltd. 253 Asoke, 12th Flr, Sukhumvit 21 Road, Klongtoey Nua, Wattana, Bangkok 10110, Thailand • Marshall Cavendish (Malaysia) Sdn Bhd, Times Subang, Lot 46, Subang Hi-Tech Industrial Park, Batu Tiga, 40000 Shah Alam, Selangor Darul Ehsan, Malaysia

Marshall Cavendish is a trademark of Times Publishing Limited

All websites were available and accurate when this book was sent to press.

Library of Congress Cataloging-in-Publication Data

Walker, Kate.
    Plants. — 1st ed.
        p. cm. — (Investigating Earth)
    Includes index.
    Summary: "Describes what plants are and why they're important"—Provided by publisher.
    ISBN 978-1-60870-559-7
    1. Plants—Juvenile literature. 2. Plant ecology—Juvenile literature. I. Title.
    QK49.W157 2012
    580—dc22
                                                    2010044217

First published in 2011 by
MACMILLAN EDUCATION AUSTRALIA PTY LTD
15–19 Claremont Street, South Yarra 3141

Visit our website at www.macmillan.com.au or go directly to www.macmillanlibrary.com.au

Associated companies and representatives throughout the world.

Publisher: Carmel Heron
Commissioning Editor: Niki Horin
Managing Editor: Vanessa Lanaway
Editor: Helena Newton
Proofreader: Kylie Cockle

Designer: Kerri Wilson
Page layout: Romy Pearse
Photo researcher: Legend Images
Illustrator: Andrew Hopgood
Production Controller: Vanessa Johnson

Printed in China

Acknowledgments
The author and publisher are grateful to the following for permission to reproduce copyright material:

Front cover photograph: Boy carrying seedlings © Corbis/Ronnie Kaufman/Larry Hirshowitz/Blend Images.

Photographs courtesy of: Corbis/Ronnie Kaufman/Larry Hirshowitz/Blend Images, 1, /MM Productions, 8; Dreamstime.com/Angelogila, 11 (center), /Chiyacat, 4 (center left), 18 (right above), /Clearviewstock, 25, /Ecophoto, 26, /Geoarts, 11 (bottom), /Kateleigh, 6, /Klotz, 4 (center right), 18 (right below), /Km2008, 4 (bottom left), 18 (bottom), /Nexus7, 10 (center), /Robynmac, 13 (right), /Rozaliya, 4 (bottom right), 18 (left above), /Sqback, 24, /Taseret, 5, /Ti_to_tito, 11 (top), /Tommason, 3, 10 (bottom), 19 (top); Getty Images/Nigel Cattlin, 15, /Kazuhiro Nogi/AFP, 30, /Gary John Norman, 21; iStockphoto/Eldad Carin, 12 (left), /Elena Elisseeva, 19 (bottom), /Yarinca, 4 (top); Newspix/News Ltd/Jake Nowakowski, 23; Photolibrary/Rob Blakers/WWI, 28, /Lineair, 19 (left), /Gabriela Staebler, 22; Shutterstock/Barbro Bergfeldt, 19 (right), /Diego Cervo, 29, /Ali Ender Birer, 18 (center), /Jake Foster, 27, /HamsterMan, 14 (right), /HLPhoto, 14 (left), /irabel8, 13 (left), /Tamara Kulikova, 12 (right), /Susan McKenzie, 4 (bottom center), 18 (left below), /Galushko Sergey, 4 (center), 18 (top), /Elena Sherengovskaya, 20, /somchaij, 10 (top).

While every care has been taken to trace and acknowledge copyright, the publisher tenders their apologies for any accidental infringement where copyright has proved untraceable. They would be pleased to come to a suitable arrangement with the rightful owner in each case.

135642

Contents

When a word is printed in **bold**, you can look up its meaning in the Glossary on page 31.

Investigating Earth

We investigate Earth to find out what makes it work. Earth is made from natural features. Some of these natural features are living and some are nonliving things.

By investigating Earth we can learn about how it works.

| Plants | Air | Rocks |
| Soil | Water | Weather |

Plants

Plants are a natural feature of Earth. They grow on land and in water. Most plants grow out of soil and almost all plants grow leaves.

trees

bushes

flowering plants

grasses

Plants include trees, bushes, flowering plants and grasses.

What Are Plants?

Plants are living things that grow in one place. Plants make their own food from the materials around them.

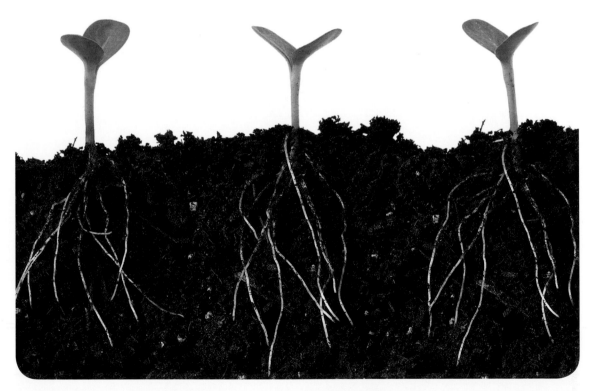

Plants grow by making food from materials in the air and the soil.

Plants can have four main parts. Each part of a plant does a special job.

Many plants have four main parts that have different jobs.

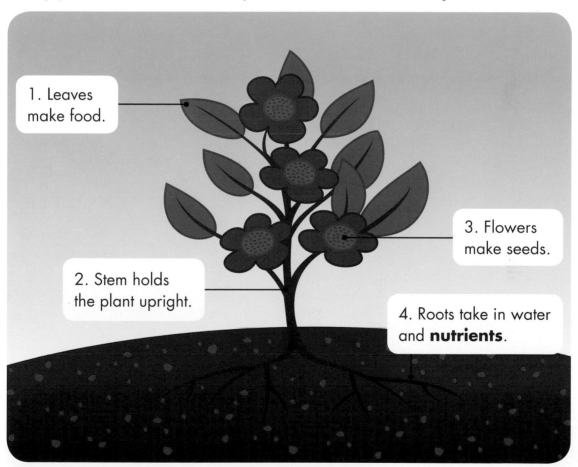

1. Leaves make food.

2. Stem holds the plant upright.

3. Flowers make seeds.

4. Roots take in water and **nutrients**.

What Are Plants Made Of?

Plants are made of two main materials, water and **carbon**. Plants get water from the soil. They get carbon by taking in **carbon dioxide gas** from the air.

Plants take in water from the soil around them.

Plants use energy from sunlight to turn water and carbon dioxide into food. This process is called **photosynthesis**.

Plants use energy from sunlight to mix carbon, water, and nutrients to make food.

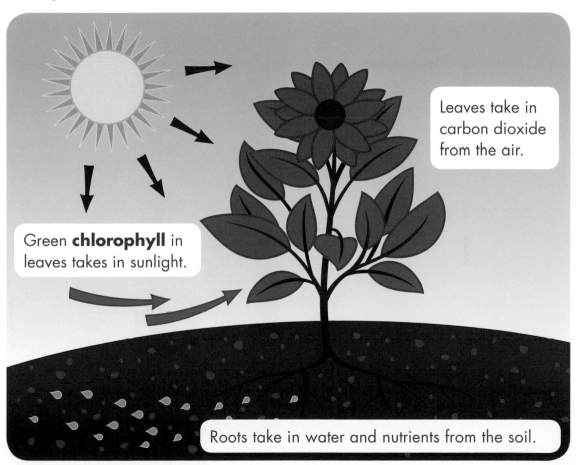

Leaves take in carbon dioxide from the air.

Green **chlorophyll** in leaves takes in sunlight.

Roots take in water and nutrients from the soil.

Different Types of Plants

There are three main types of plants on Earth.

The three main types of plants

1. Flowering plants

2. Cone-bearing plants

3. Ferns

These three different types of plants **reproduce** in different ways.

seed

flower

1. Flowering plants reproduce from seeds made inside flowers.

seed

cone

2. Cone-bearing plants reproduce from seeds made inside of **cones**.

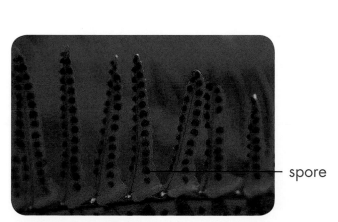

spore

3. Ferns reproduce from **spores**.

Flowering Plants

All flowering plants produce seeds. The seeds grow inside the flowers. As the flower dies, the seeds fall to the ground. New plants grow from the seeds.

seed

Seeds from an agapanthus flower fall as the flower wilts.

living agapanthus

Some flowering plants grow fruit to protect their seeds. The fruit grows inside a flower. As the flower dies, the fruit ripens. The plant seeds are protected inside the fruit.

passionfruit flower

passionfruit

The flowers of the passionfruit vine grow into passionfruit that contain seeds.

Cone-bearing Plants

Cone-bearing plants grow woodland fruit called cones, but do not grow flowers. Cones fall to the ground and open their scales to release the seeds inside. New plants grow from the seeds.

pine tree cone
with closed scales

pine tree cone
with open scales

Pine tree cones have layers
of scales with seeds inside.

seed

Ferns

Ferns have no flowers or fruit. Ferns make tiny spores that fall to the ground and grow into new ferns.

Millions of tiny spores grow in clusters on the undersides of fern leaves.

fern leaf

spore cluster

Earth's Plant Cycle

New plants grow using material left by dead plants in Earth's plant cycle.

1. A plant seed grows by taking heat, water, and nutrients from the soil. It puts down roots and sends up a single stem called a **shoot**.

shoot

4. The dead plant falls onto the soil and **decomposes**. Decomposing plants put nutrients back into the soil. Seeds get buried under the soil.

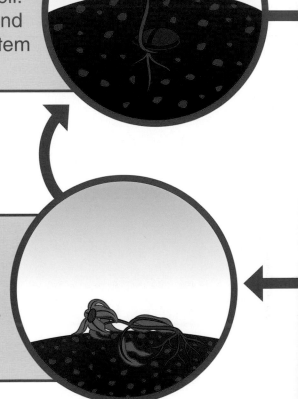

Plants use the same material over and over in Earth's plant cycle.

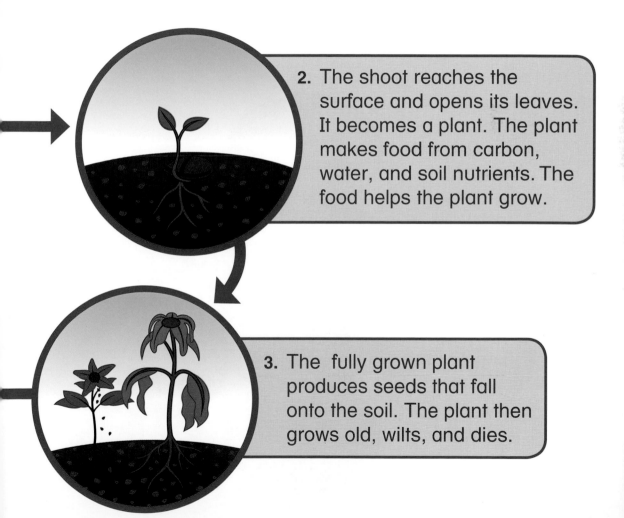

2. The shoot reaches the surface and opens its leaves. It becomes a plant. The plant makes food from carbon, water, and soil nutrients. The food helps the plant grow.

3. The fully grown plant produces seeds that fall onto the soil. The plant then grows old, wilts, and dies.

Why Are Plants Important?

Plants grow almost everywhere on Earth. Plants work together with some of Earth's other natural features. This helps to keep Earth healthy.

Earth has six main natural features that work together to keep Earth healthy.

Air

Weather

Plants

Earth

Water

Rocks

Soil

Plants work together with air and soil. They also help animals and humans survive.

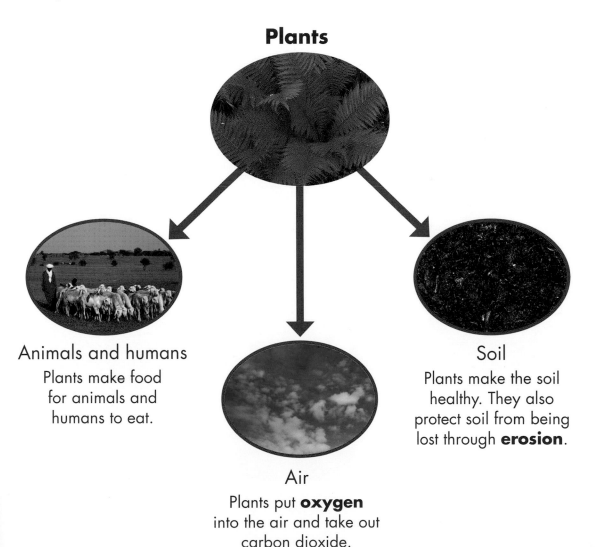

Plants

Animals and humans
Plants make food
for animals and
humans to eat.

Air
Plants put **oxygen**
into the air and take out
carbon dioxide.

Soil
Plants make the soil
healthy. They also
protect soil from being
lost through **erosion**.

Plants Feed Animals and Humans

Plants produce food that animals and humans need to eat. Humans eat many different types of plants, such as fruits and vegetables. Most other animals eat one or two types.

Grazing animals, such as cows, need to eat grass to survive.

Some animals and humans eat meat. Plants are also important to meat eaters. This is because most meat comes from animals that once ate plants.

People eat meat and eggs from chickens. Chickens need to eat plant foods, such as wheat and corn.

Plants Put Oxygen Into the Air

Plants take in carbon dioxide and give off oxygen. Most of the oxygen in the air comes from plants. Animals and humans must breathe in oxygen from the air to survive.

All animals need to breathe oxygen from plants.

Some human activities put carbon dioxide into the air. Too much carbon dioxide in the air can cause problems. Plants help remove carbon dioxide by turning it into oxygen.

Planting more trees helps remove carbon dioxide from the air.

Plants Make the Soil Healthy

Plants help make the soil healthy by putting nutrients into the soil when they die. Dead plants fall onto the soil and decompose.

Healthy soil contains the organic material that was in plants when they were alive.

Worms, beetles, and other soil-dwelling animals eat organic material, break it up, and turn it into nutrients. Soil-dwelling animals spread nutrients, air, and water through the soil as they burrow around.

Plants provide food for worms and other burrowing animals that help keep the soil healthy.

Plants Protect the Soil

Plants protect soil from erosion by water and wind. Soil is loose material that is easily washed away by running water. Plants hold soil in place with their roots.

Plants near running water help hold the soil in place with their roots.

Dry soil is light and easily blown away by wind. Plants drop **leaf litter**, which stops sunlight from drying soil. This keeps soil moist and stops it from blowing away.

— leaf litter

Leaf litter from plants covers and protects the soil underneath from the sun.

Protecting Plants

Plants are important to other living things on Earth and need to be protected. Every day humans cut down large areas of natural forest to make products such as paper.

When forests are cut down, animals that live in trees lose their homes.

We can help protect trees by using less paper. When we use less paper, fewer trees are cut down to make new paper. We can also recycle and reuse paper.

Reusing and recycling paper helps to protect trees.

Amazing Plants

One of the world's biggest plants is the giant Victoria waterlily. It grows in the Amazon River basin in South America.

The leaves of these giant water lilies can grow to 10 feet (3 meters) across and can hold a person.

Glossary

carbon   Substance found in nature and in all living things.

carbon dioxide   Gas in the air that plants take in.

chlorophyll   Green substance in plant leaves that takes in sunlight.

cones   Dry woodland fruit of cone-bearing plants, such as pine and fir trees.

decomposes   Breaks down naturally.

erosion   Breaking up and wearing away of Earth's surface by natural forces, such as water or weather.

gas   Light, floating substance, such as oxygen or carbon dioxide.

leaf litter   Dead leaves dropped by plants.

nutrients   Substances in soil that plants use to make food.

oxygen   Gas in the air that animals and humans breathe in.

photosynthesis   Process by which plants use sunlight to make food.

reproduce   Make new plants.

shoot   First small stem grown by a plant seed.

spores   Tiny parts of plants from which new plants grow.

Index